25 Unique coloring patterns with bible verse quotes

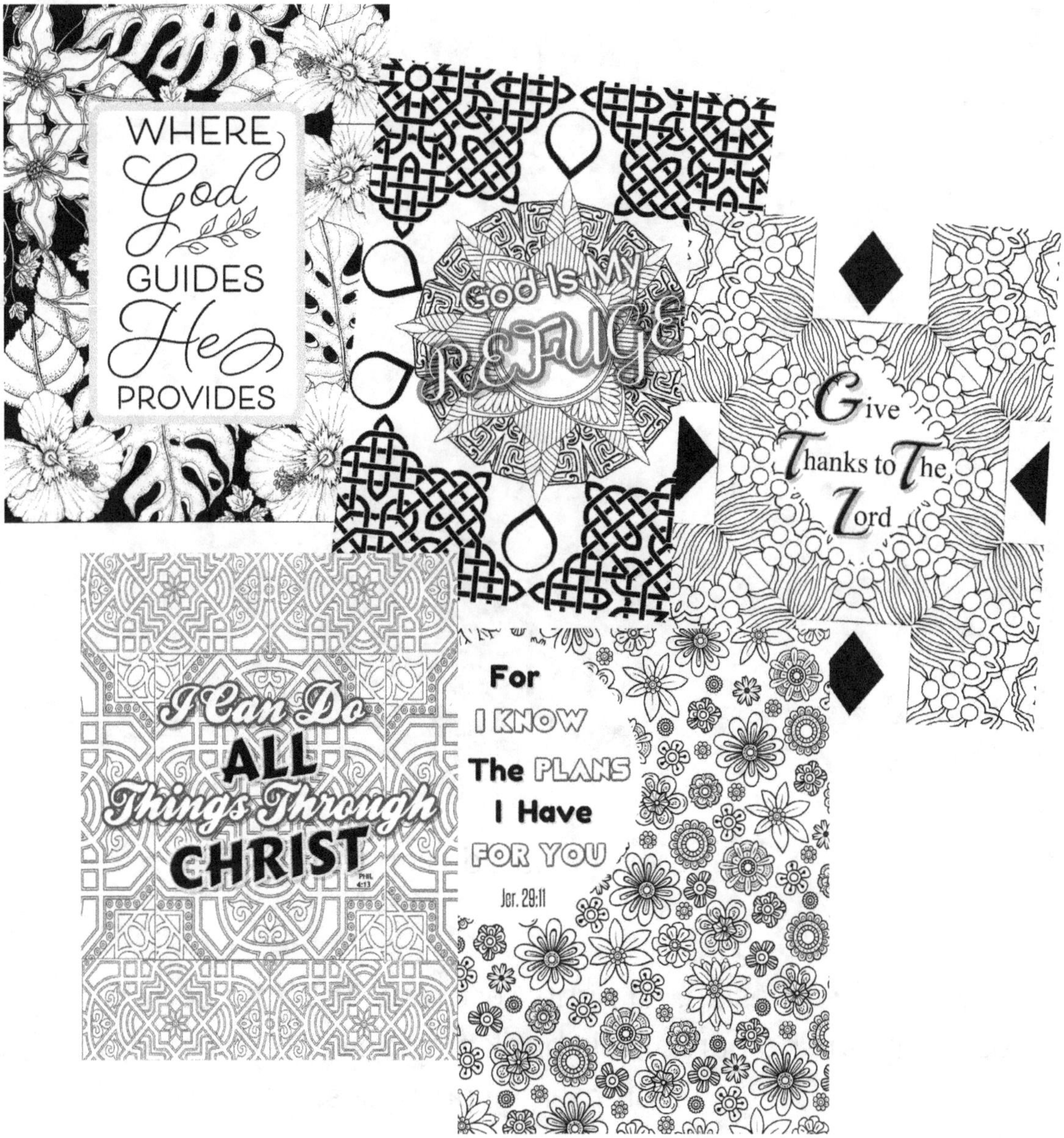

Author Name: Be Exalted Design
To see more christian paperback journals, coloring books & more

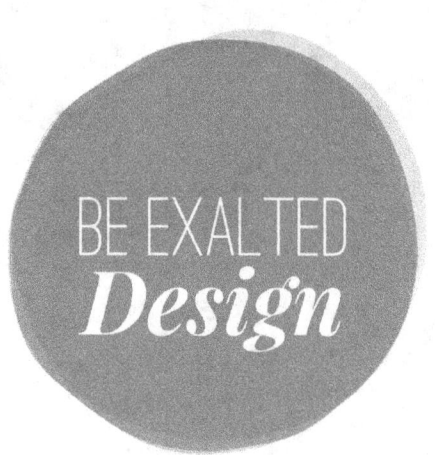

www.exalteddesign.com

©2019 Be Exalted Design. All rights reserved. This one copy is for personal use only and no part of this book may be reproduced or used for commercial purposes.

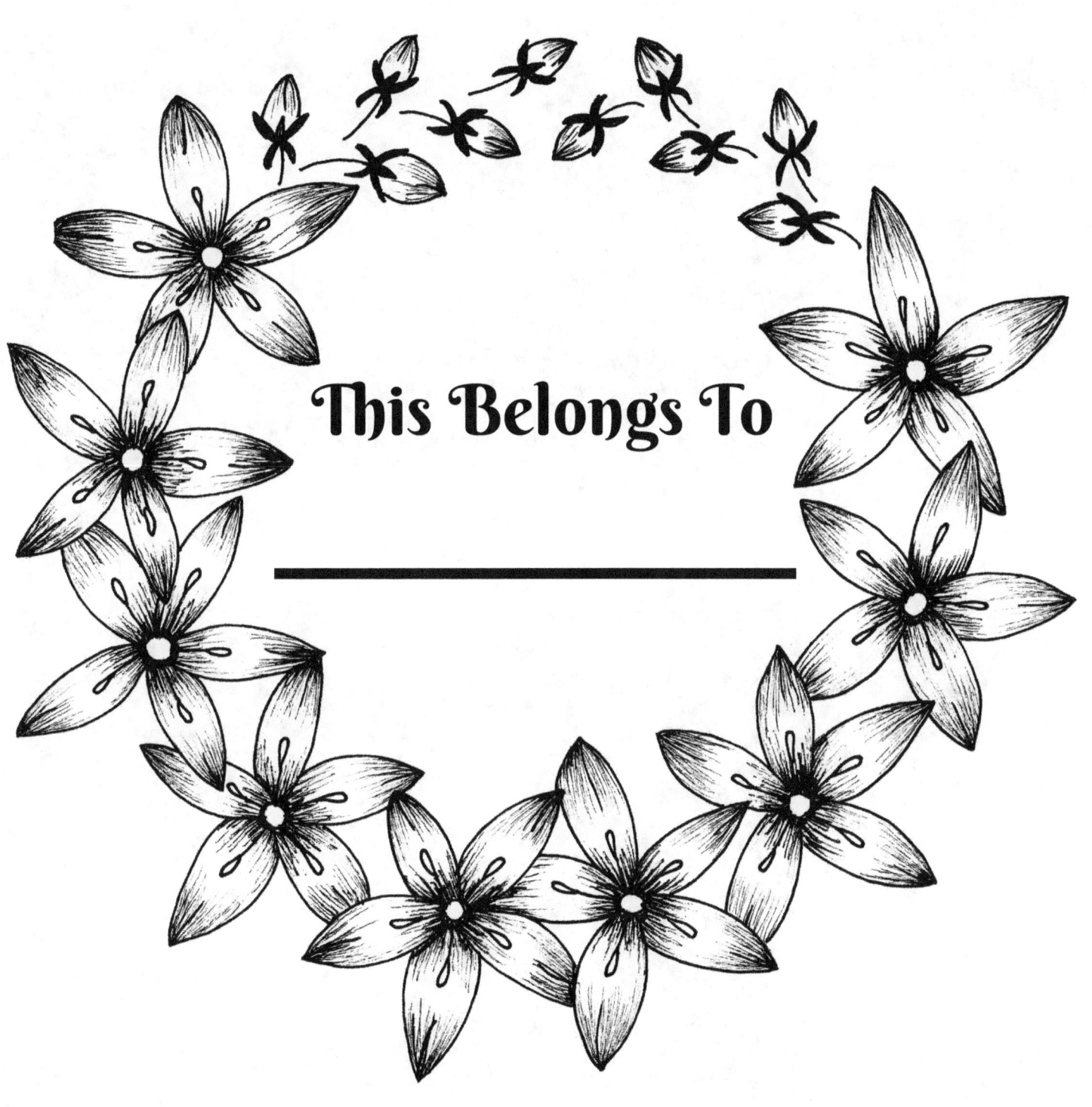

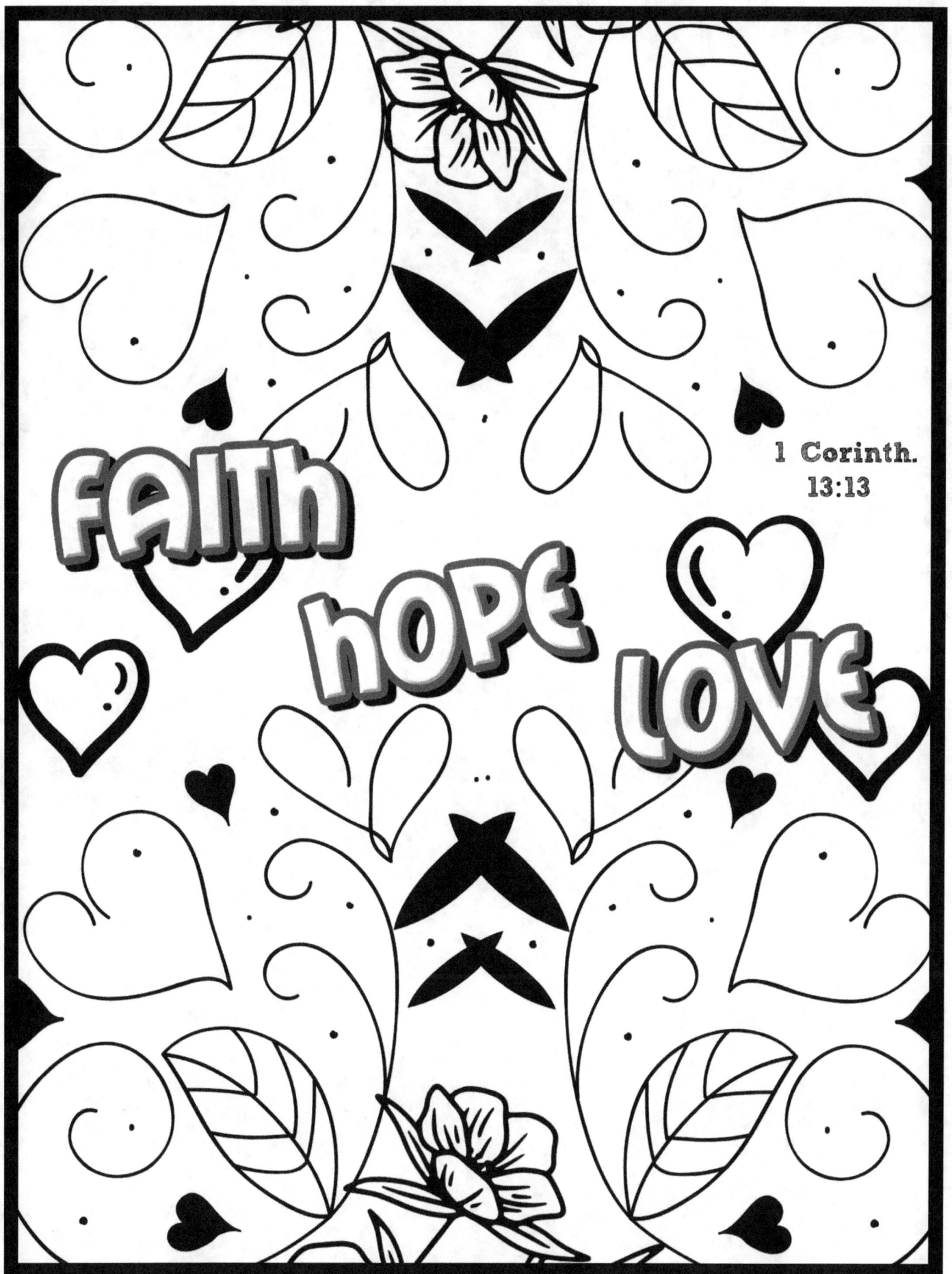

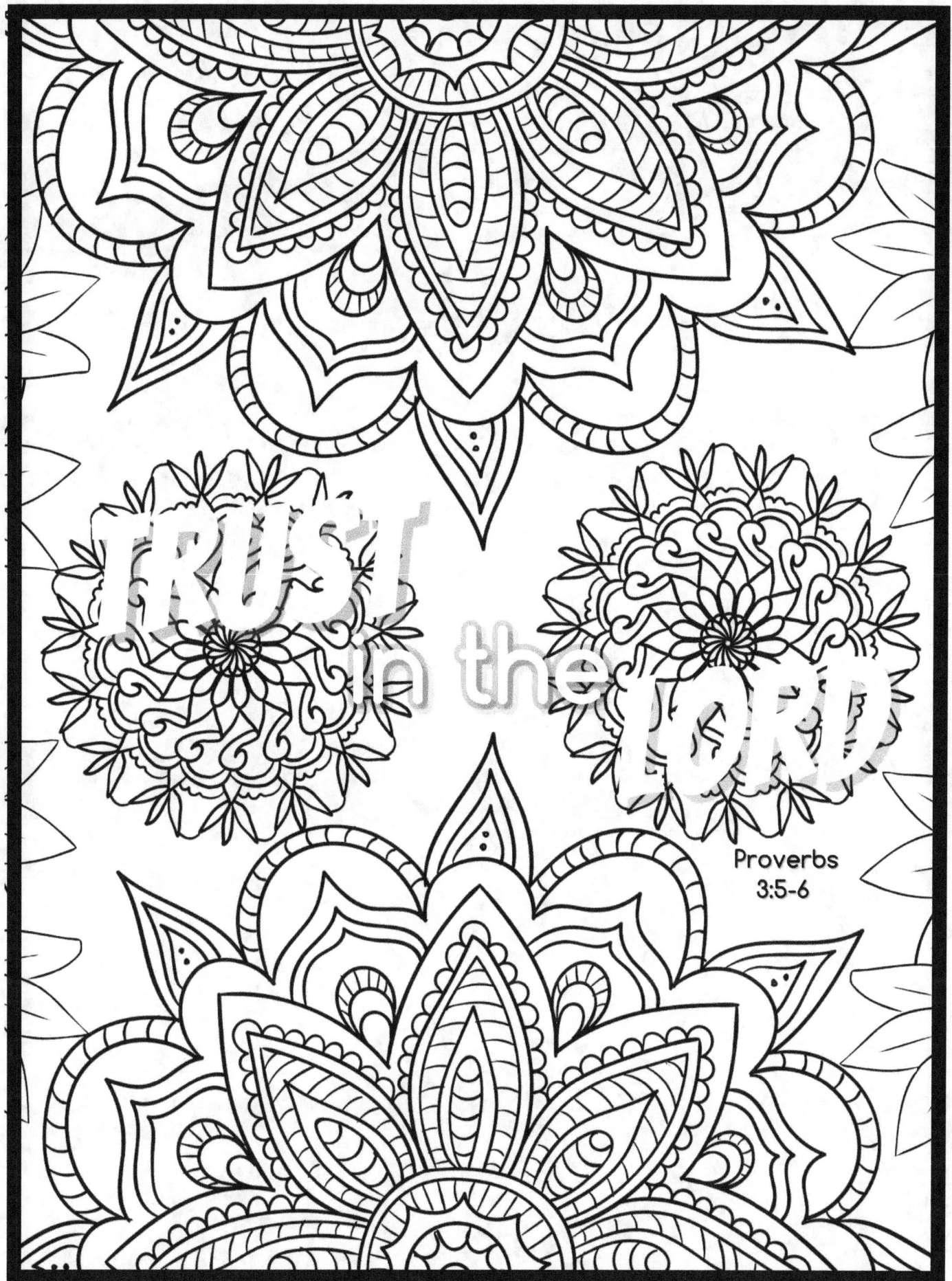

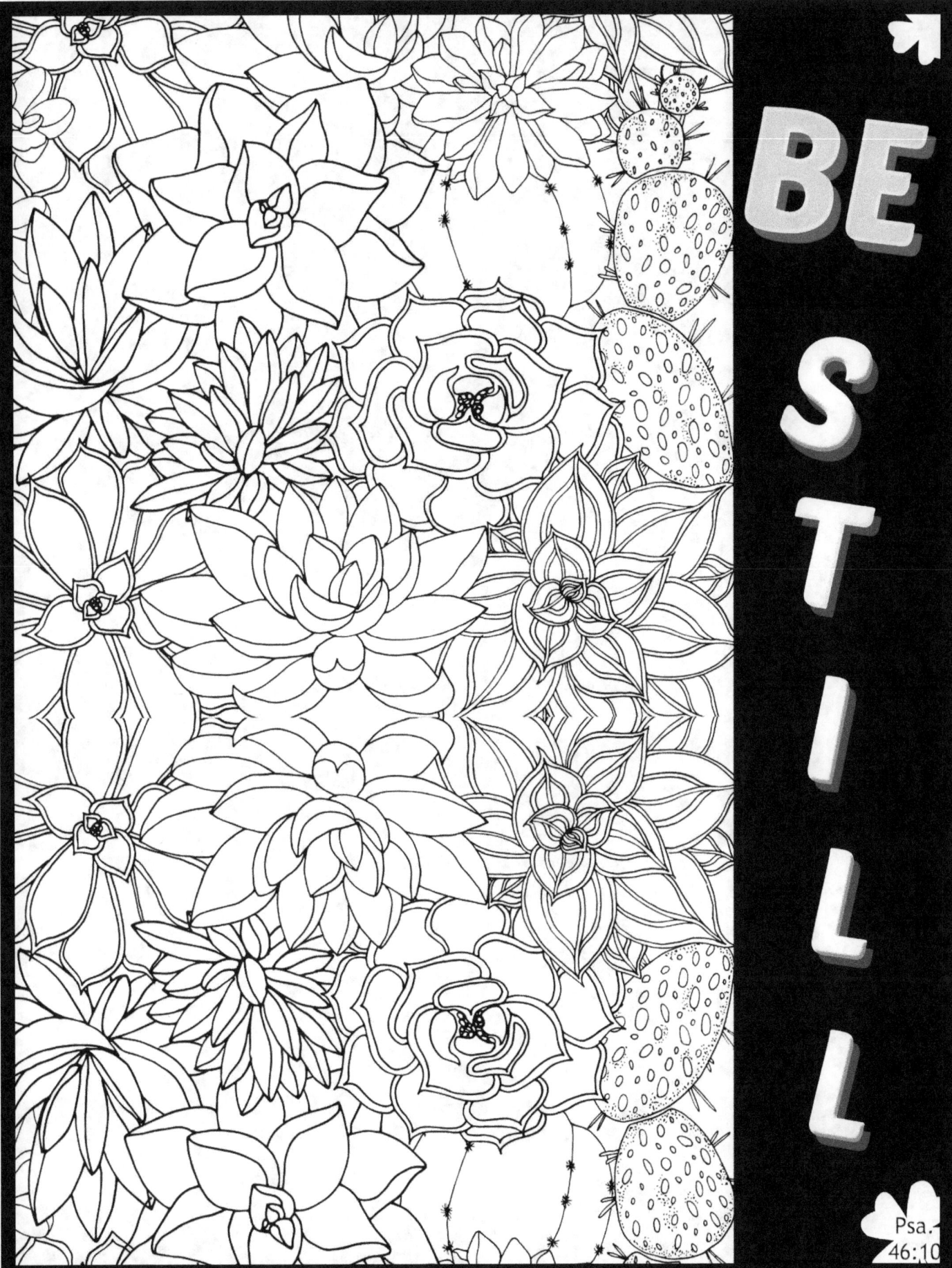

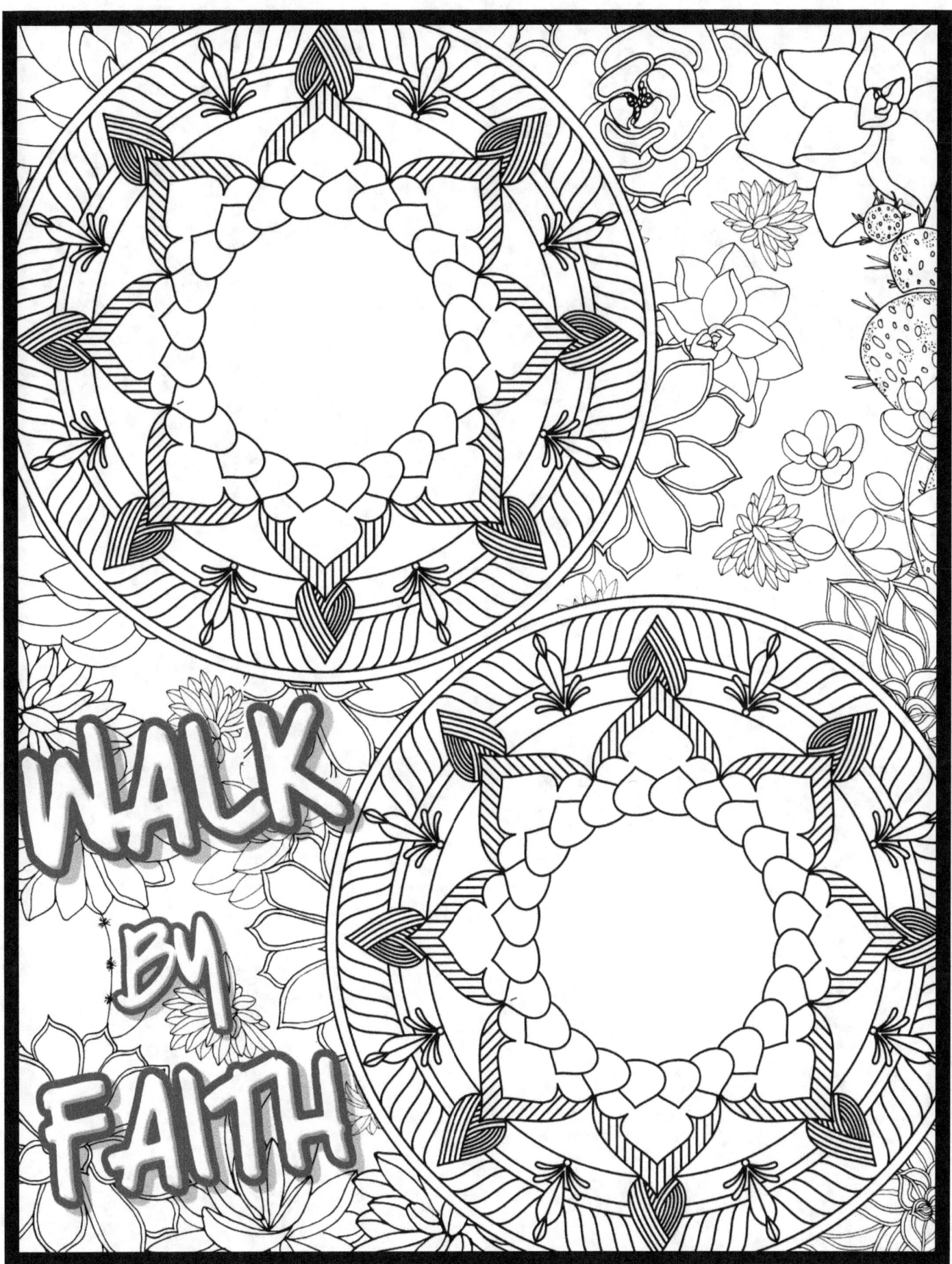

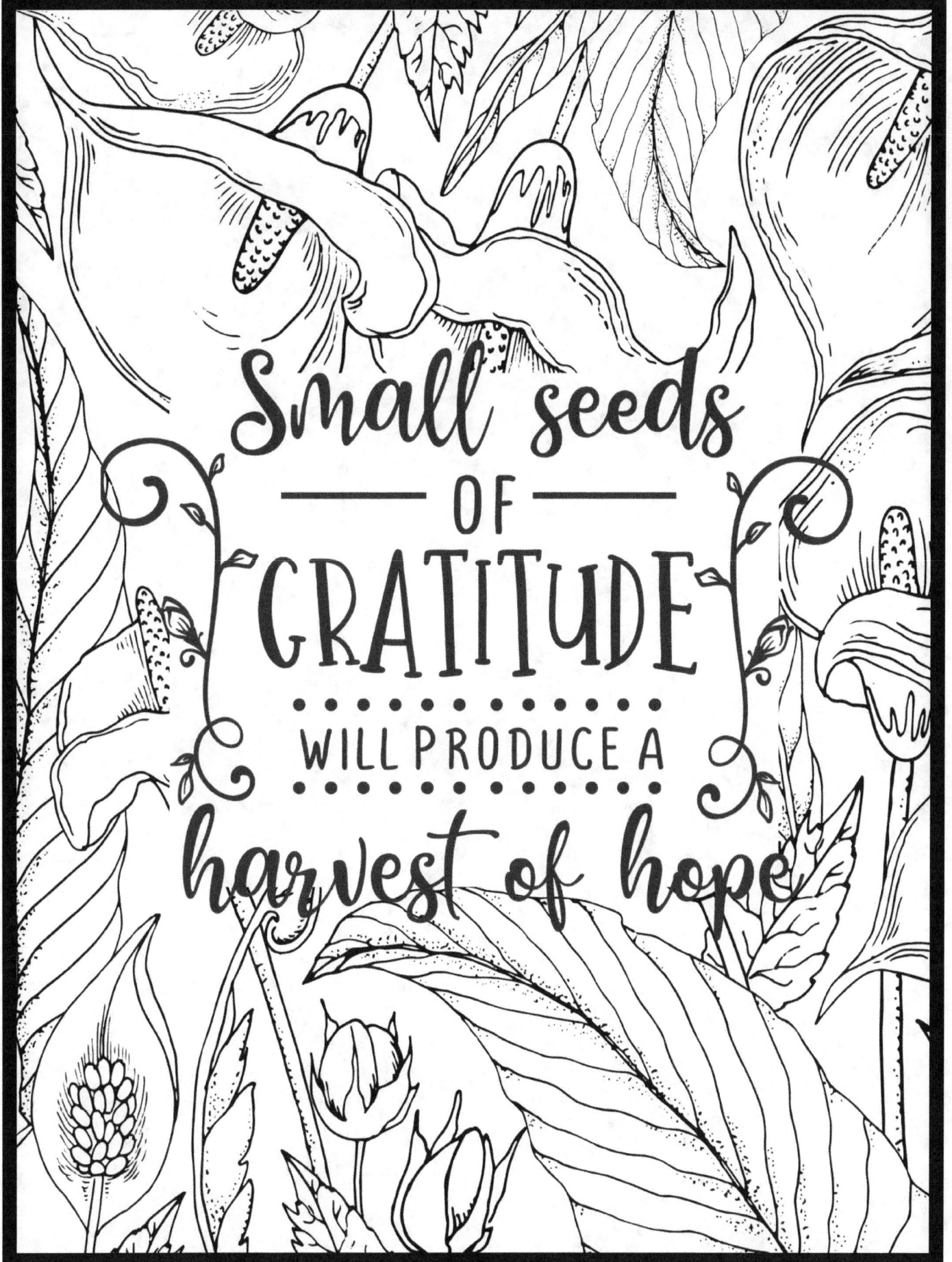

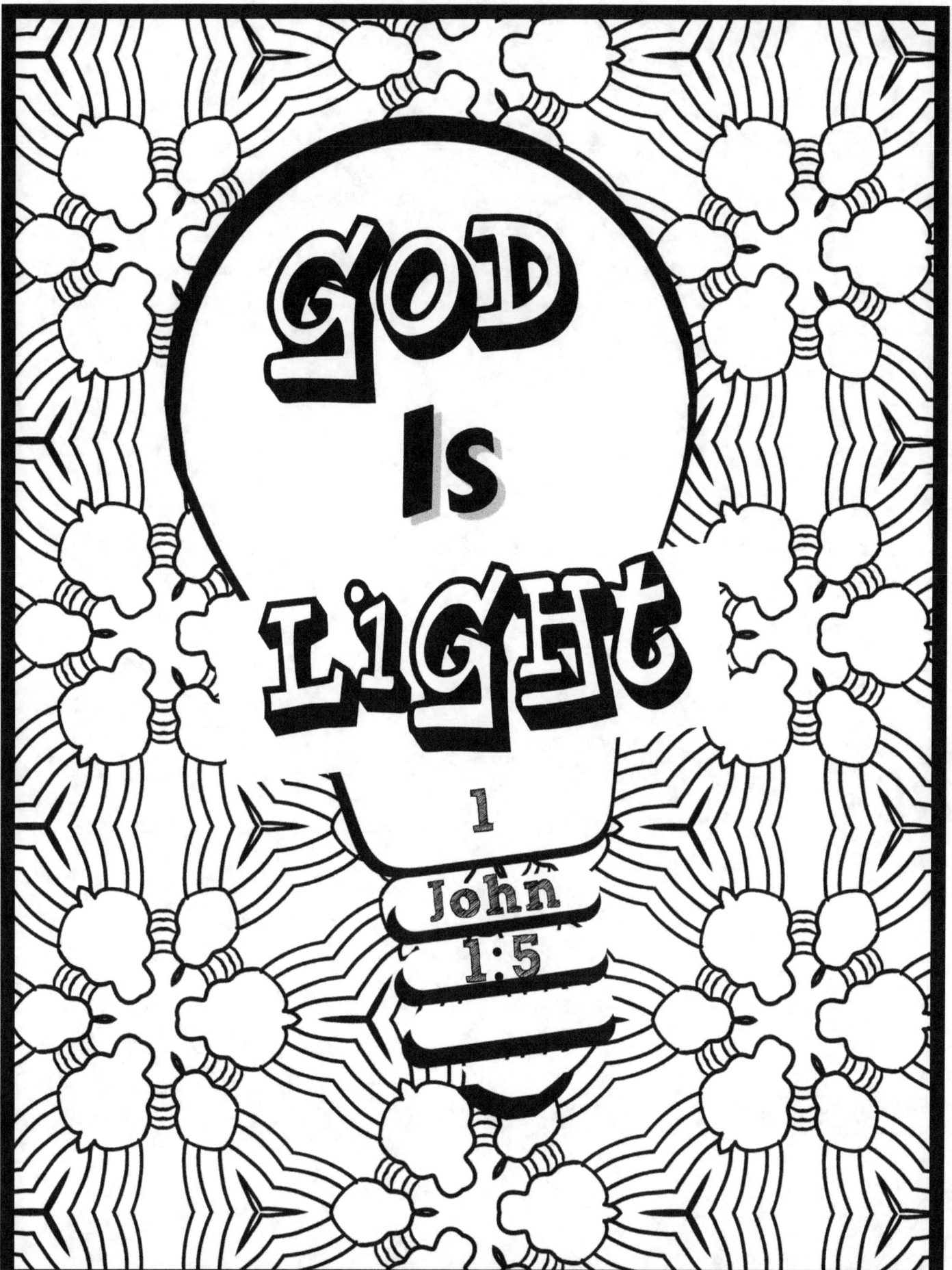

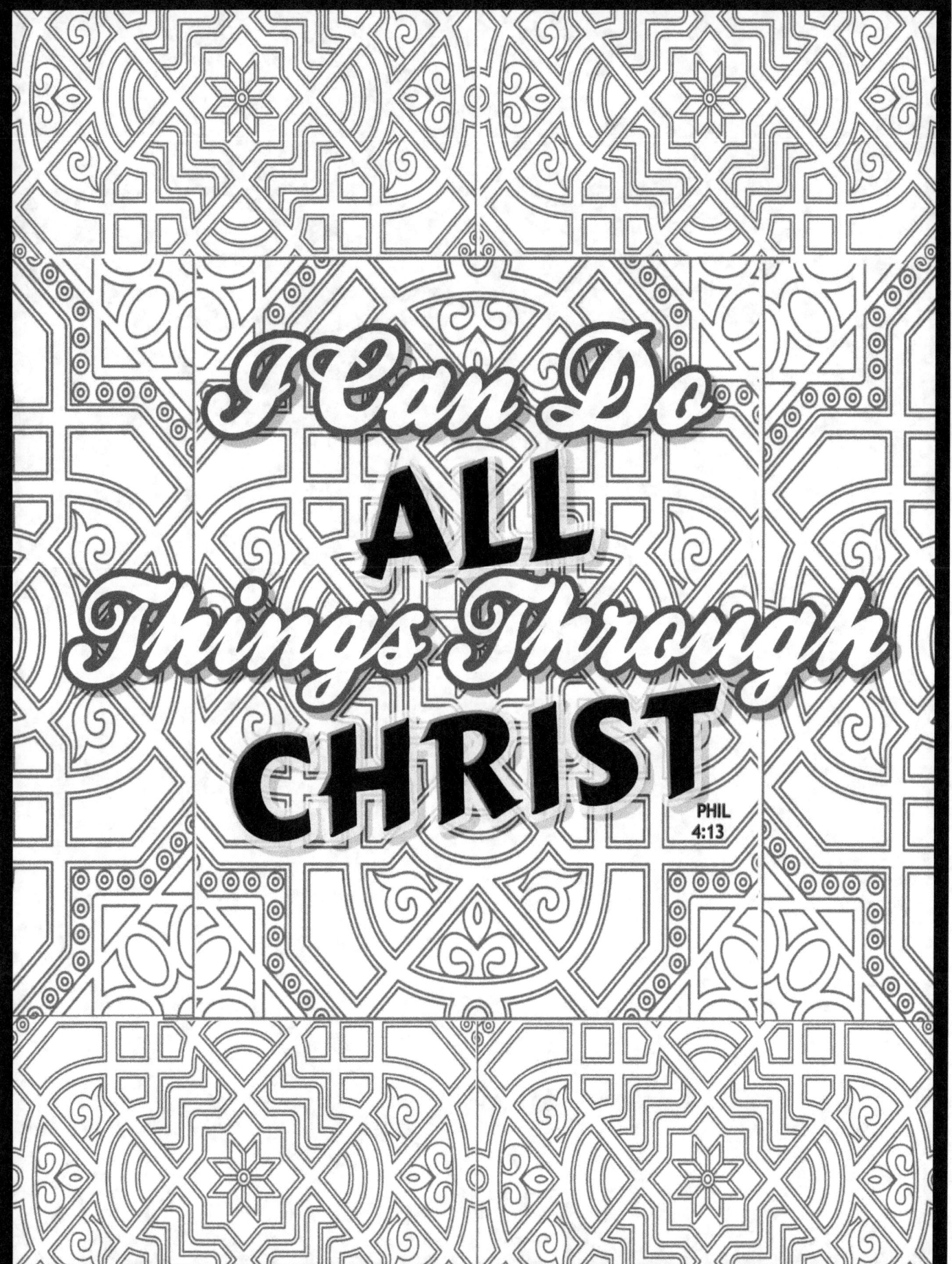

DELIGHT YOURSELF IN THE LORD

Psalm 37:4

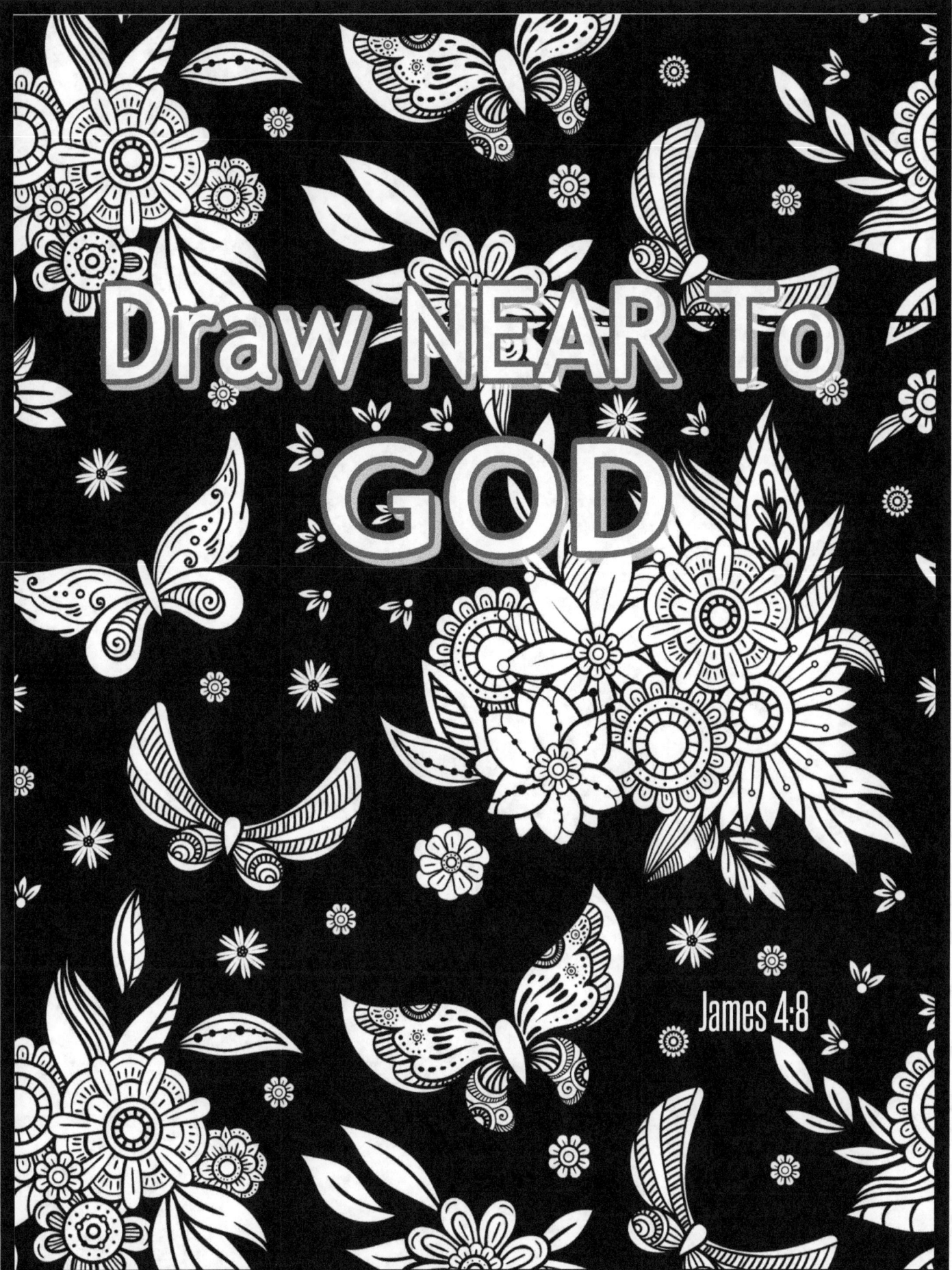

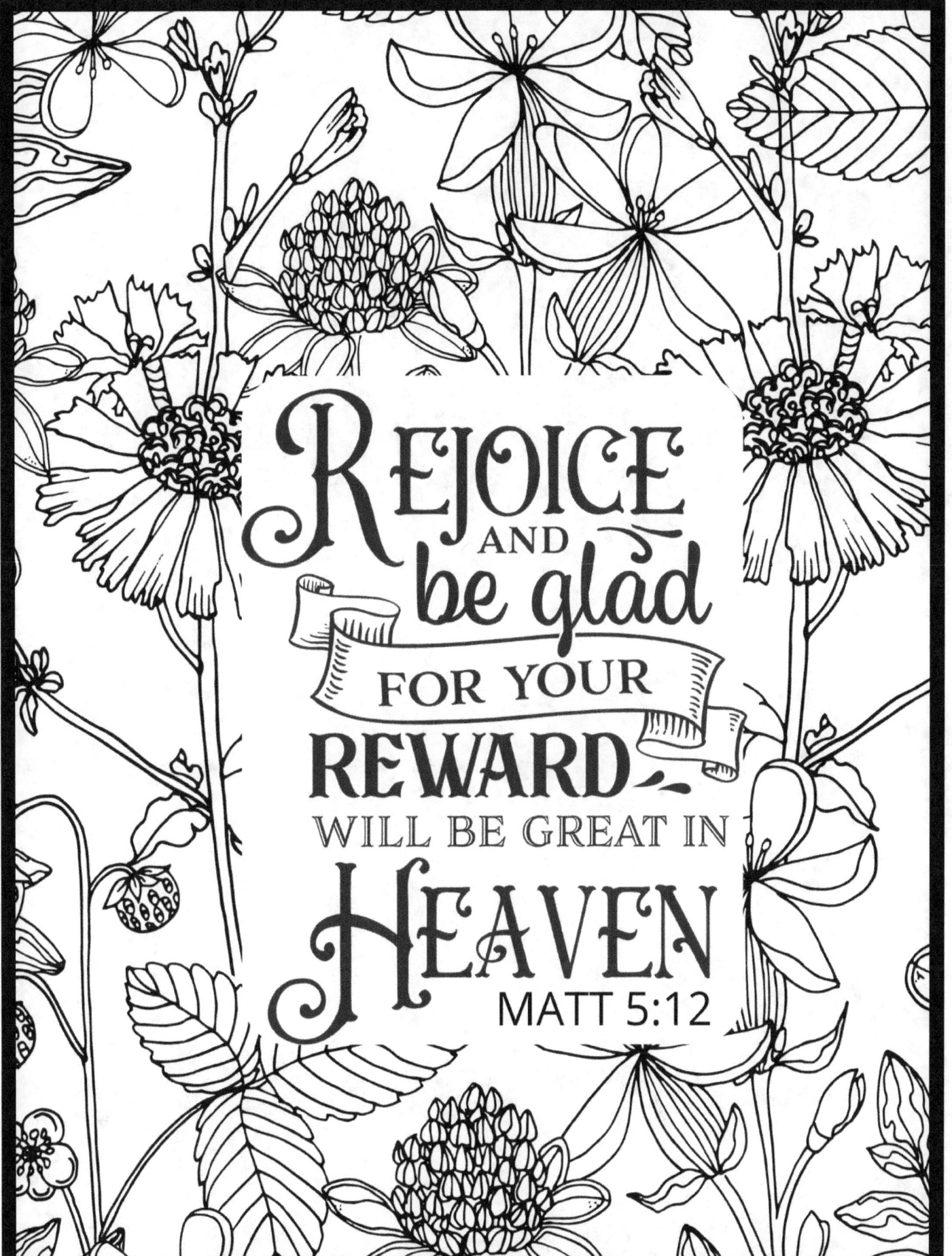

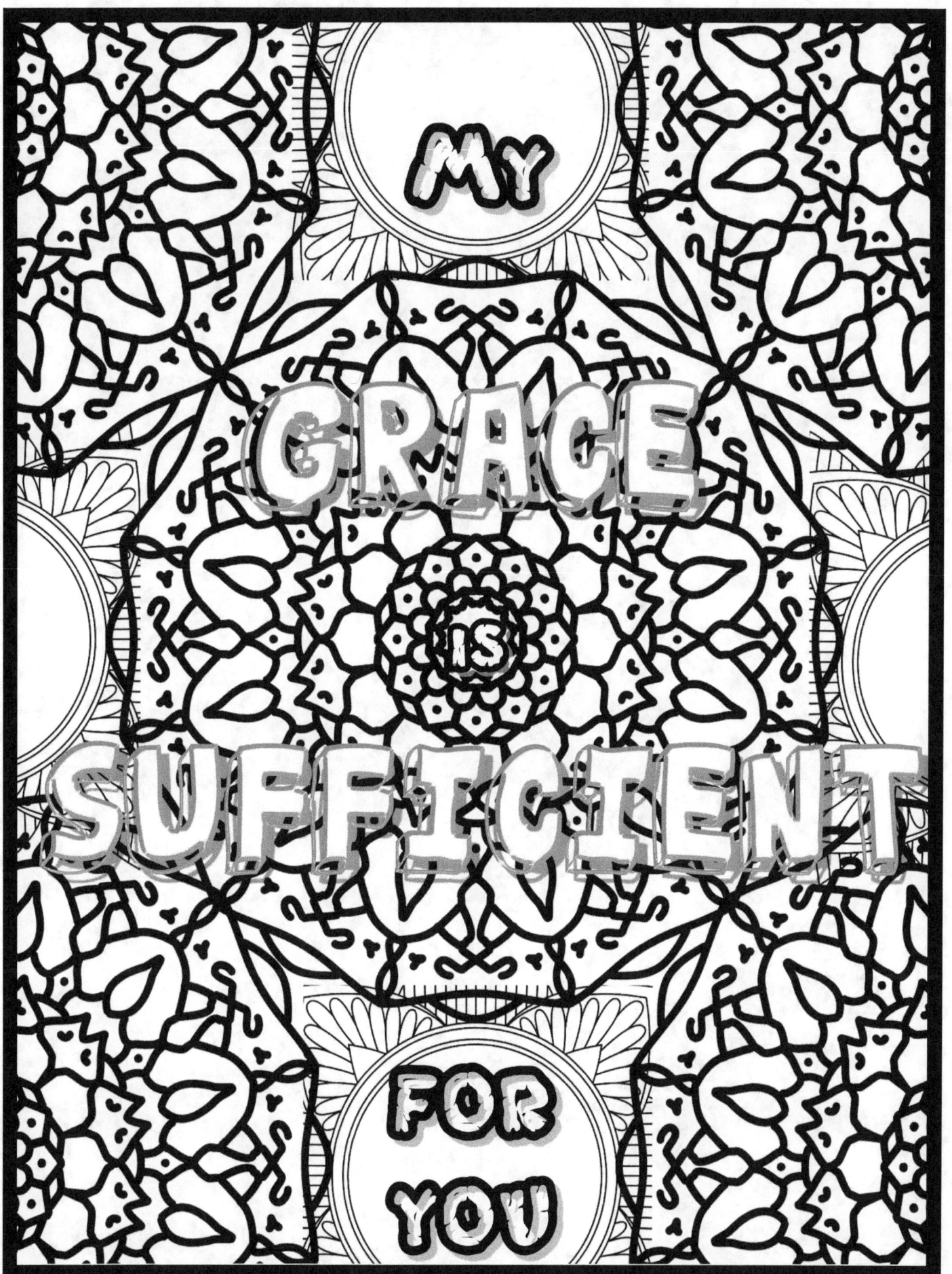

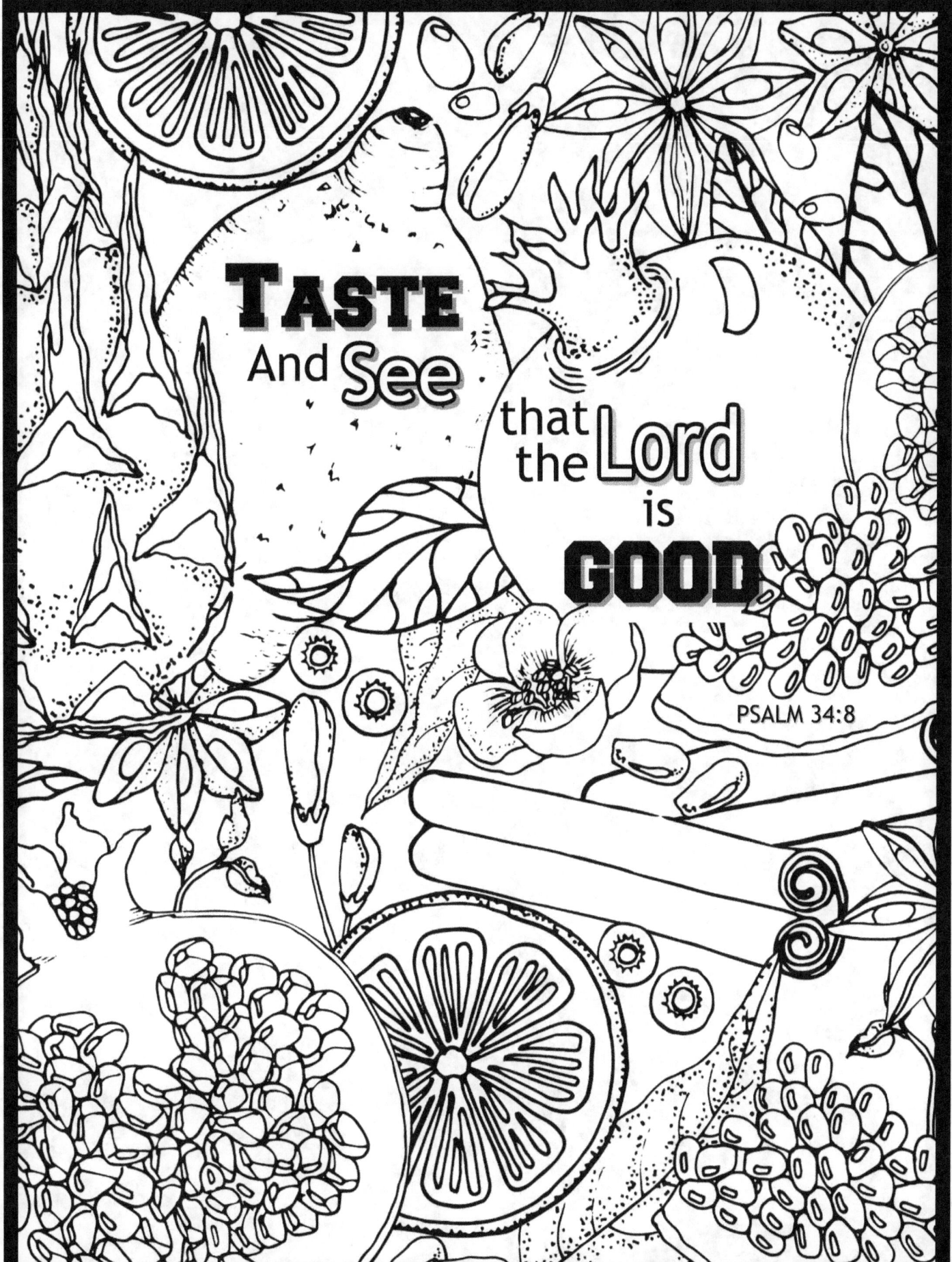

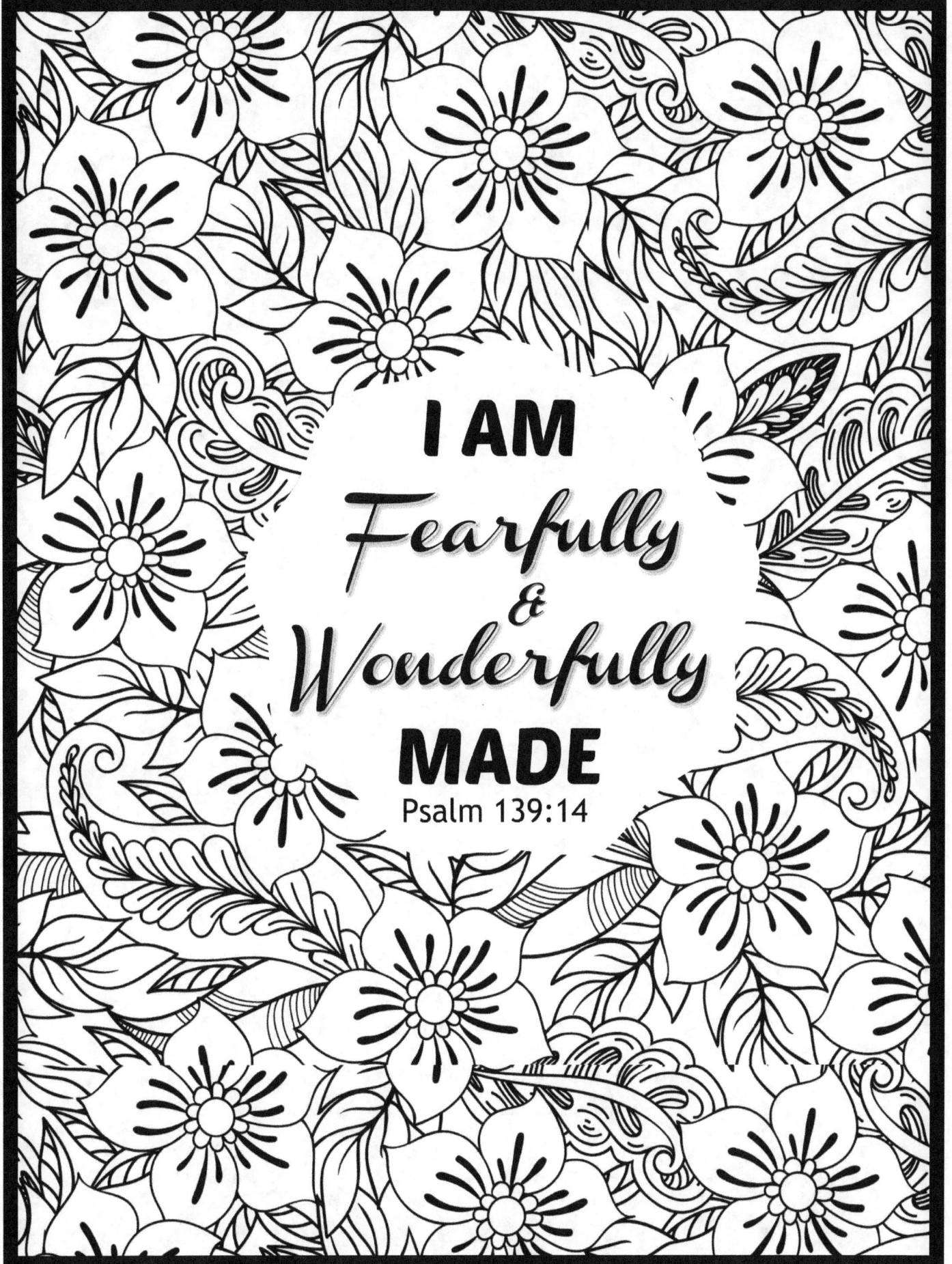

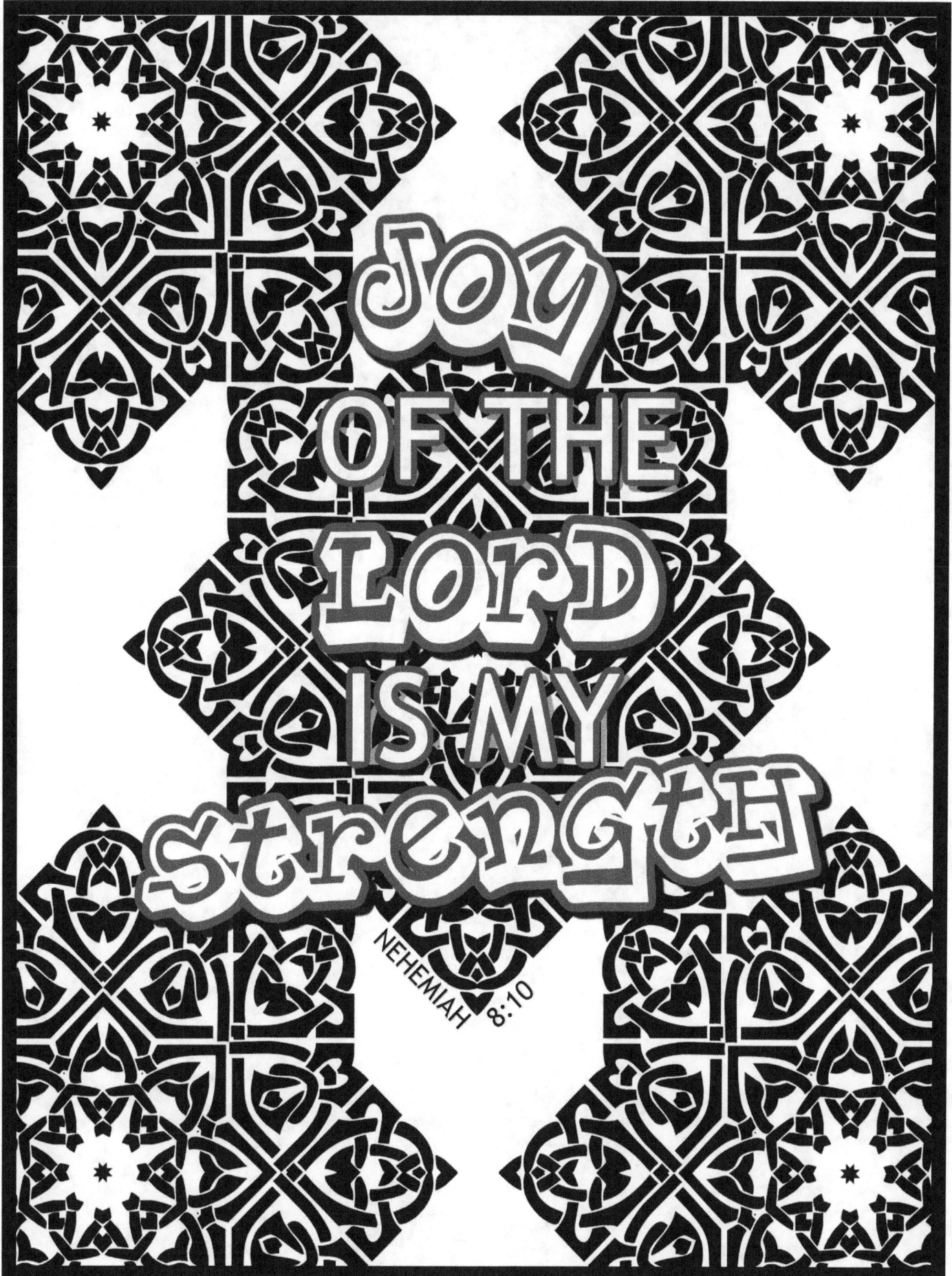

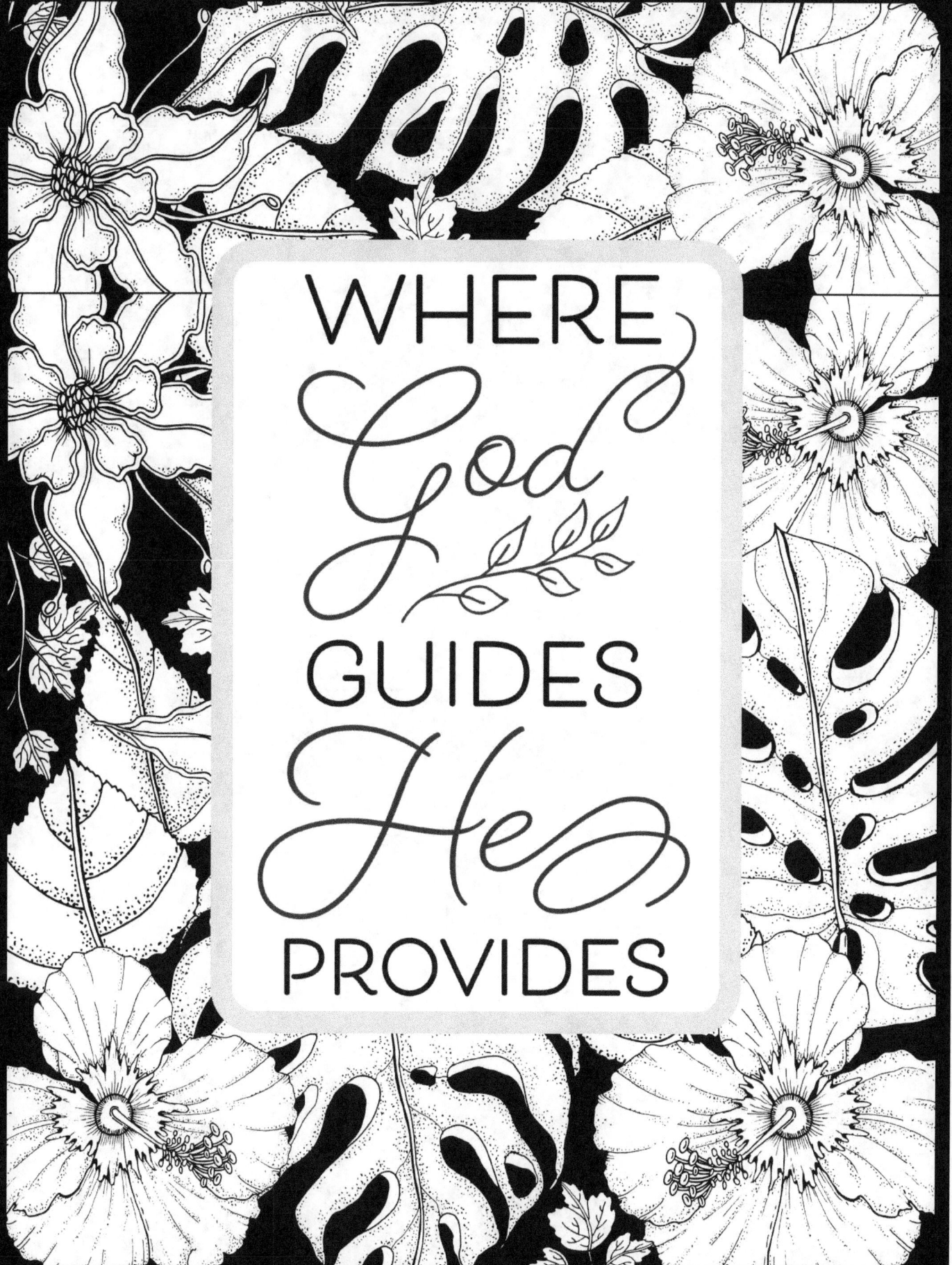

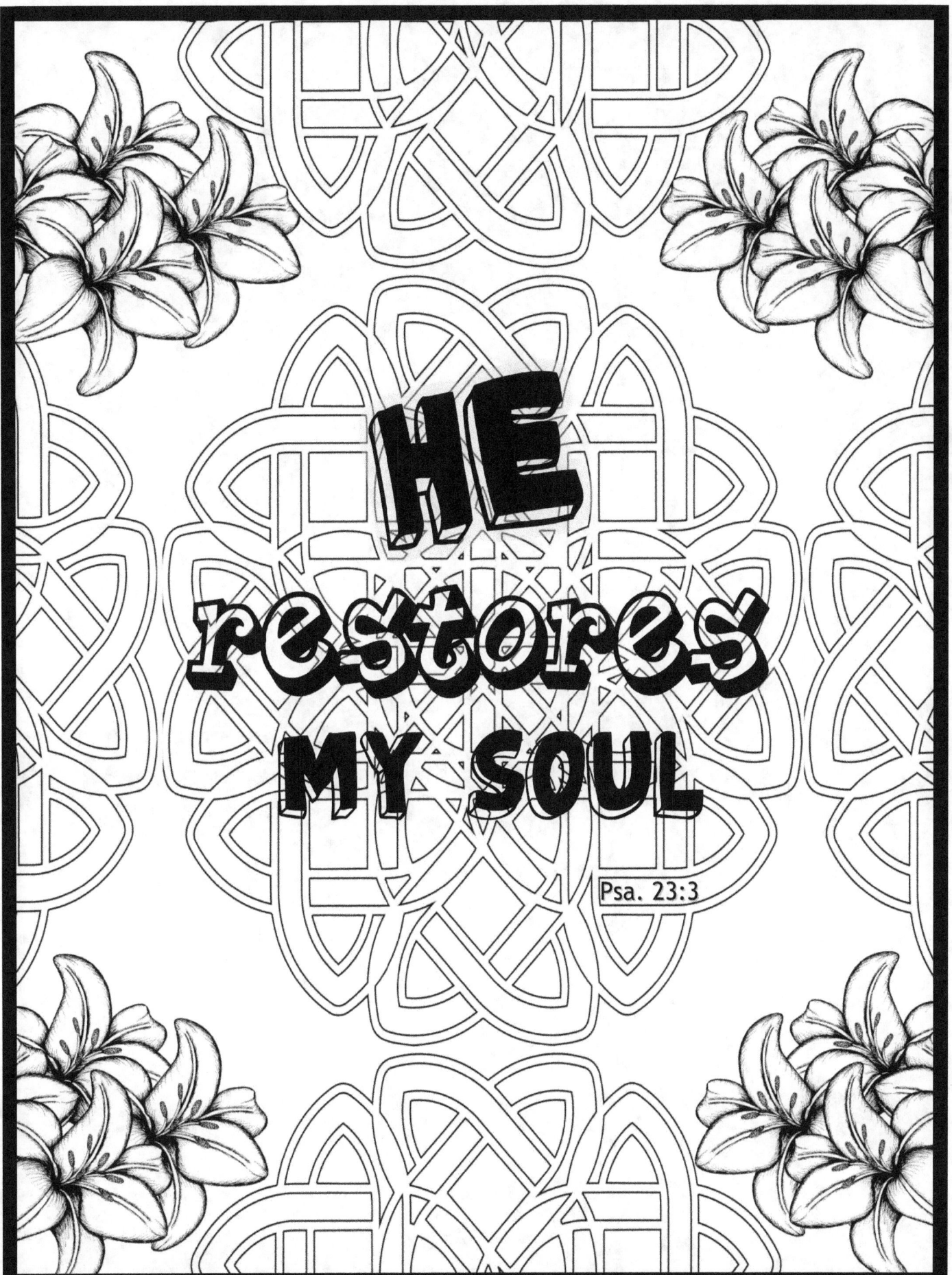

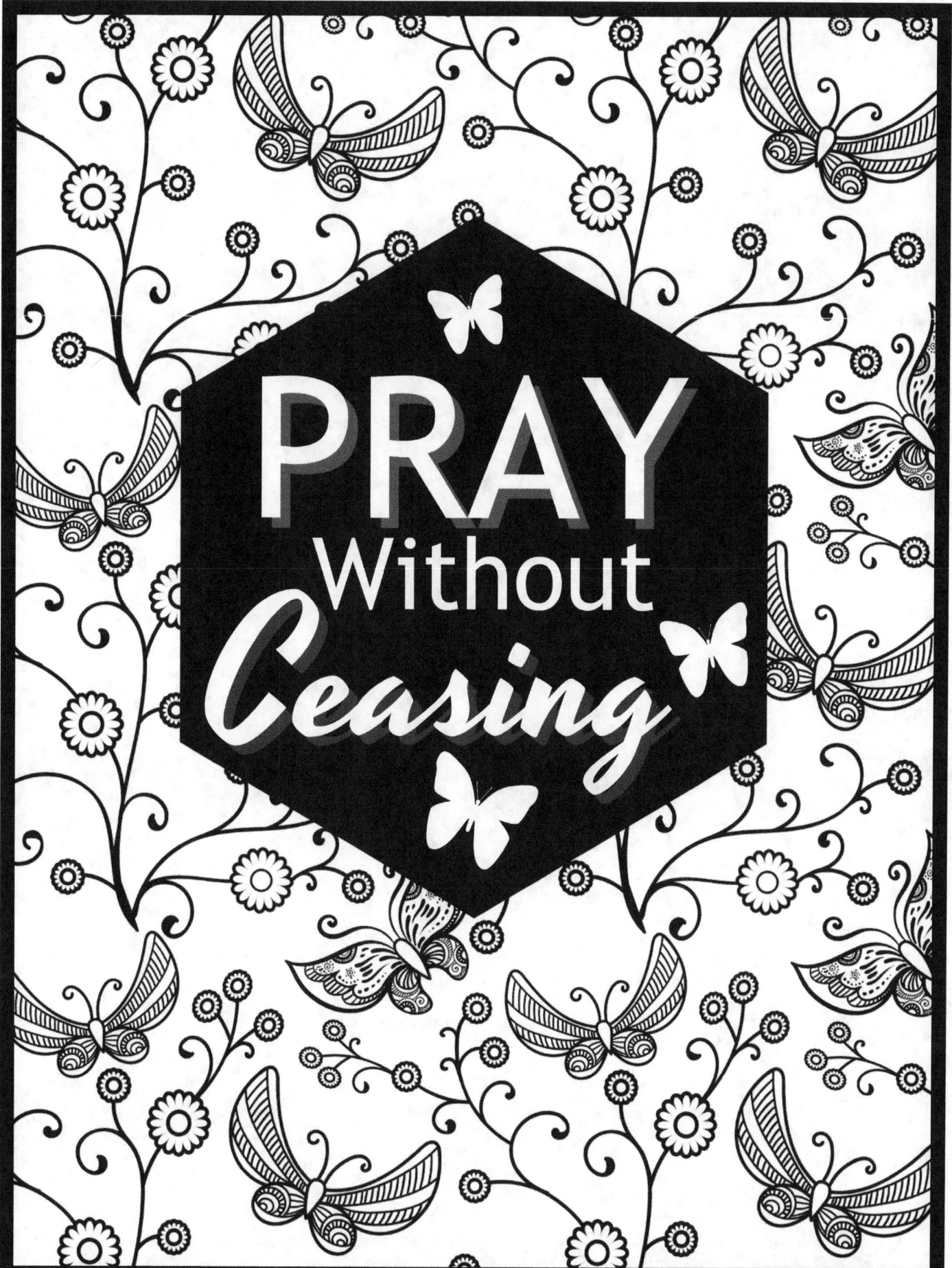

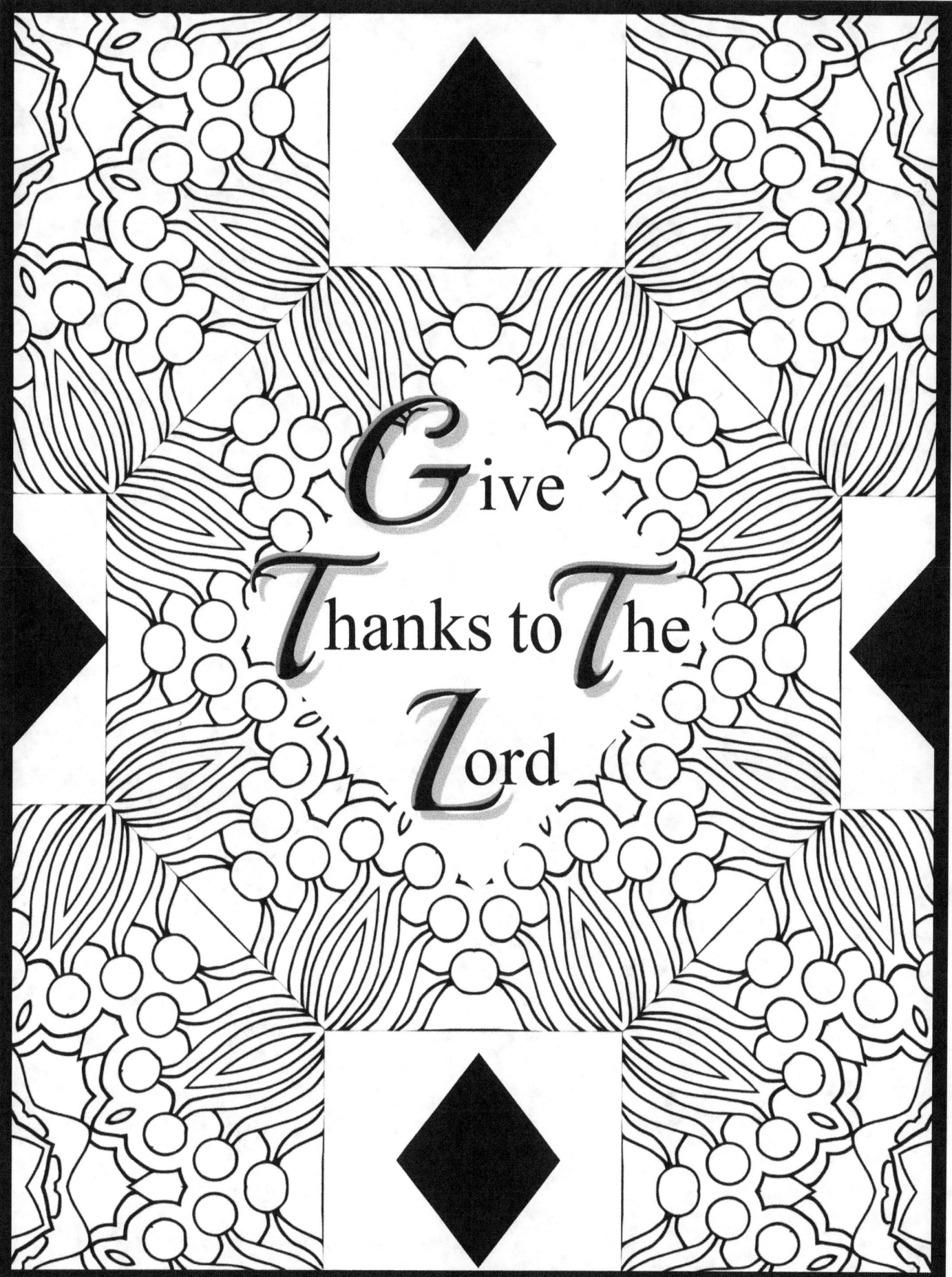

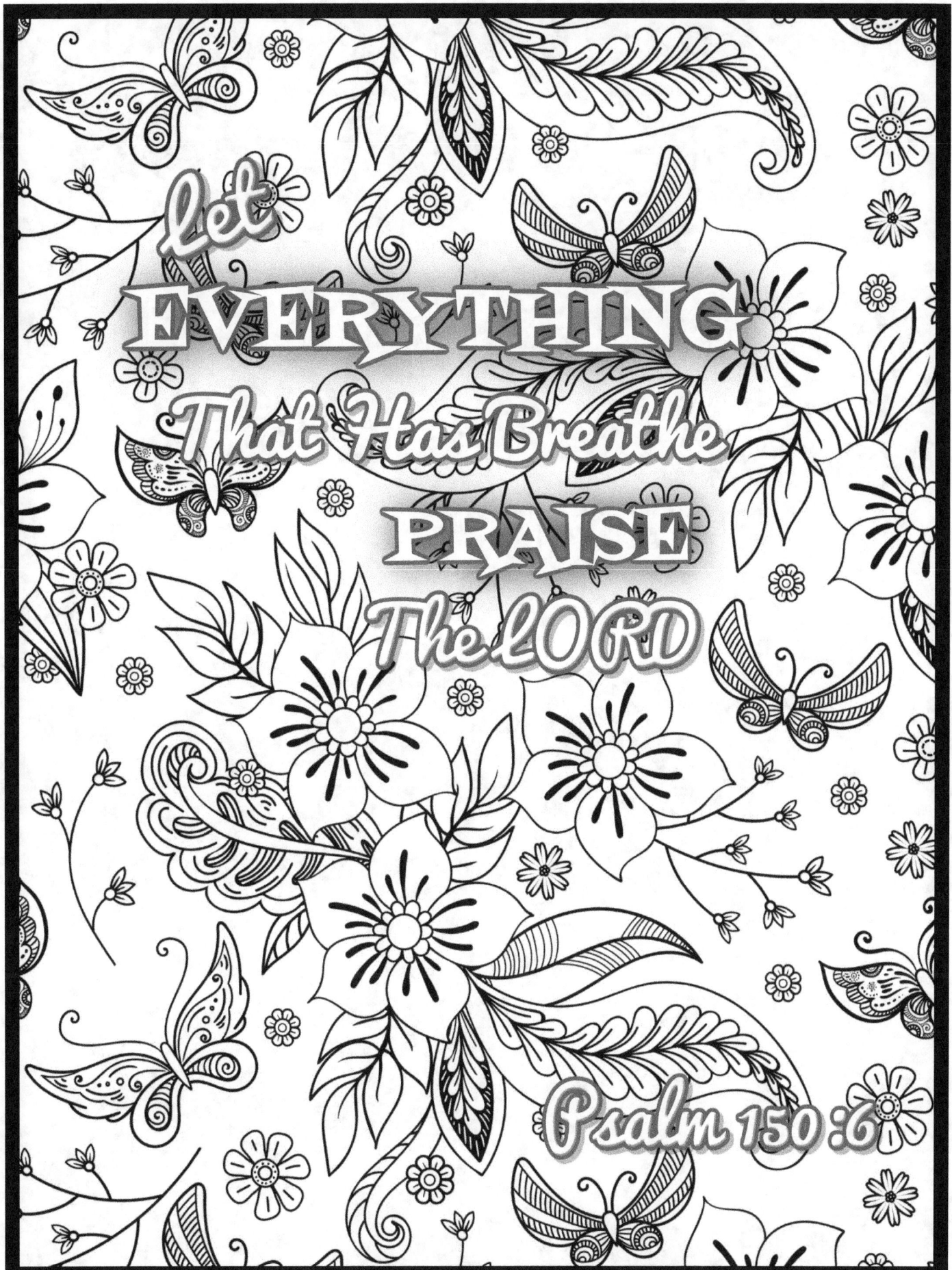

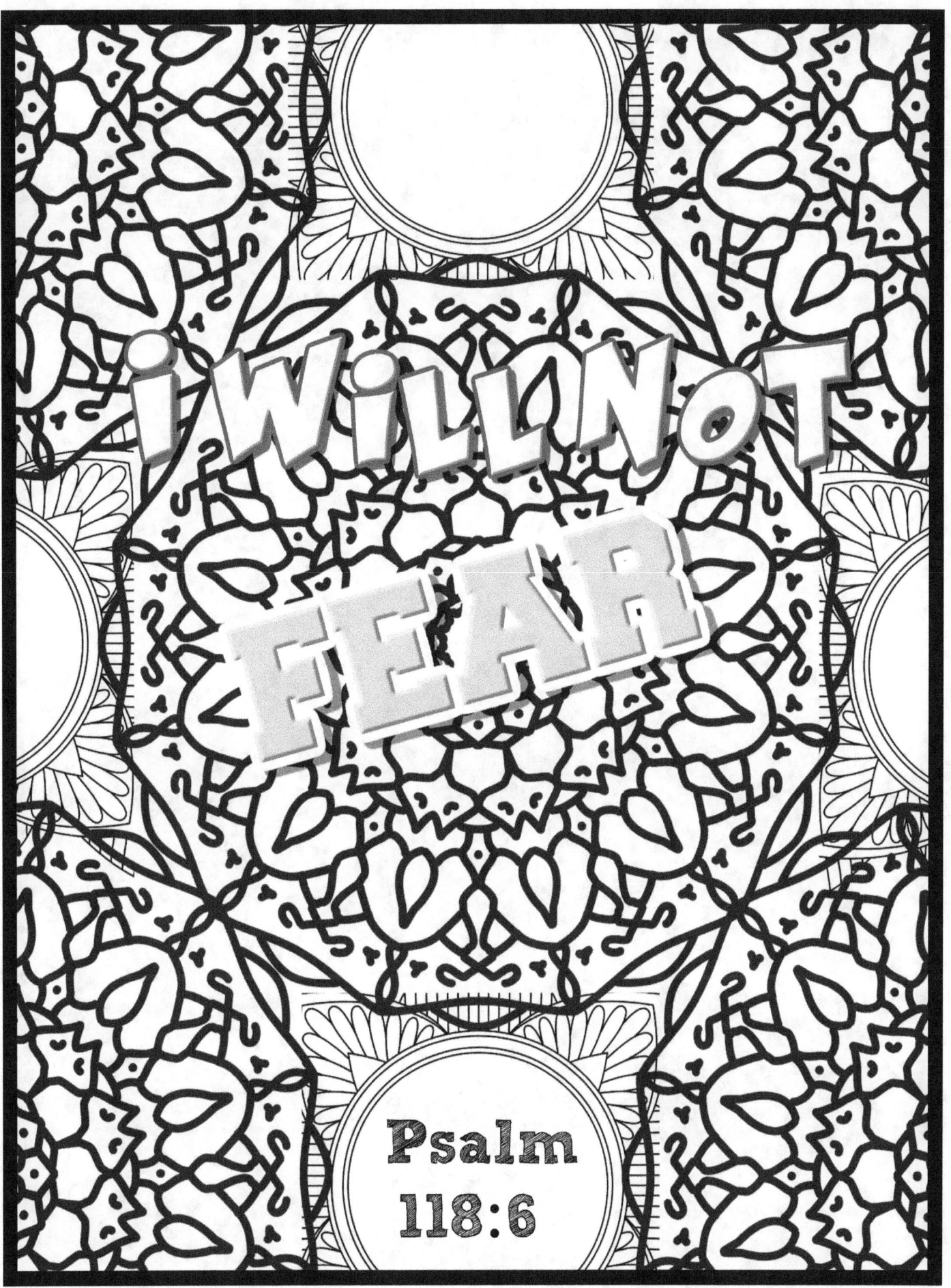

All Things Are Possible

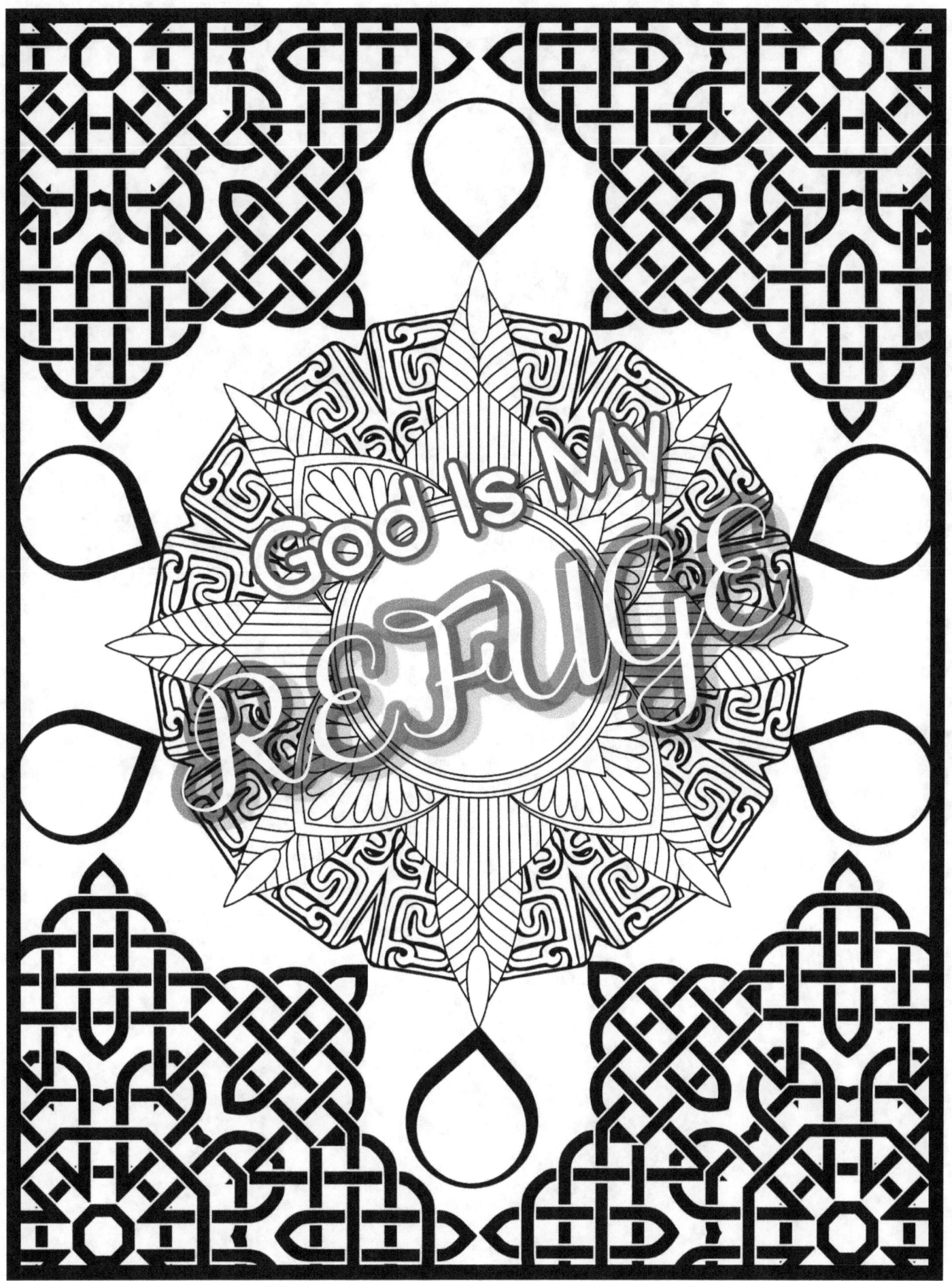

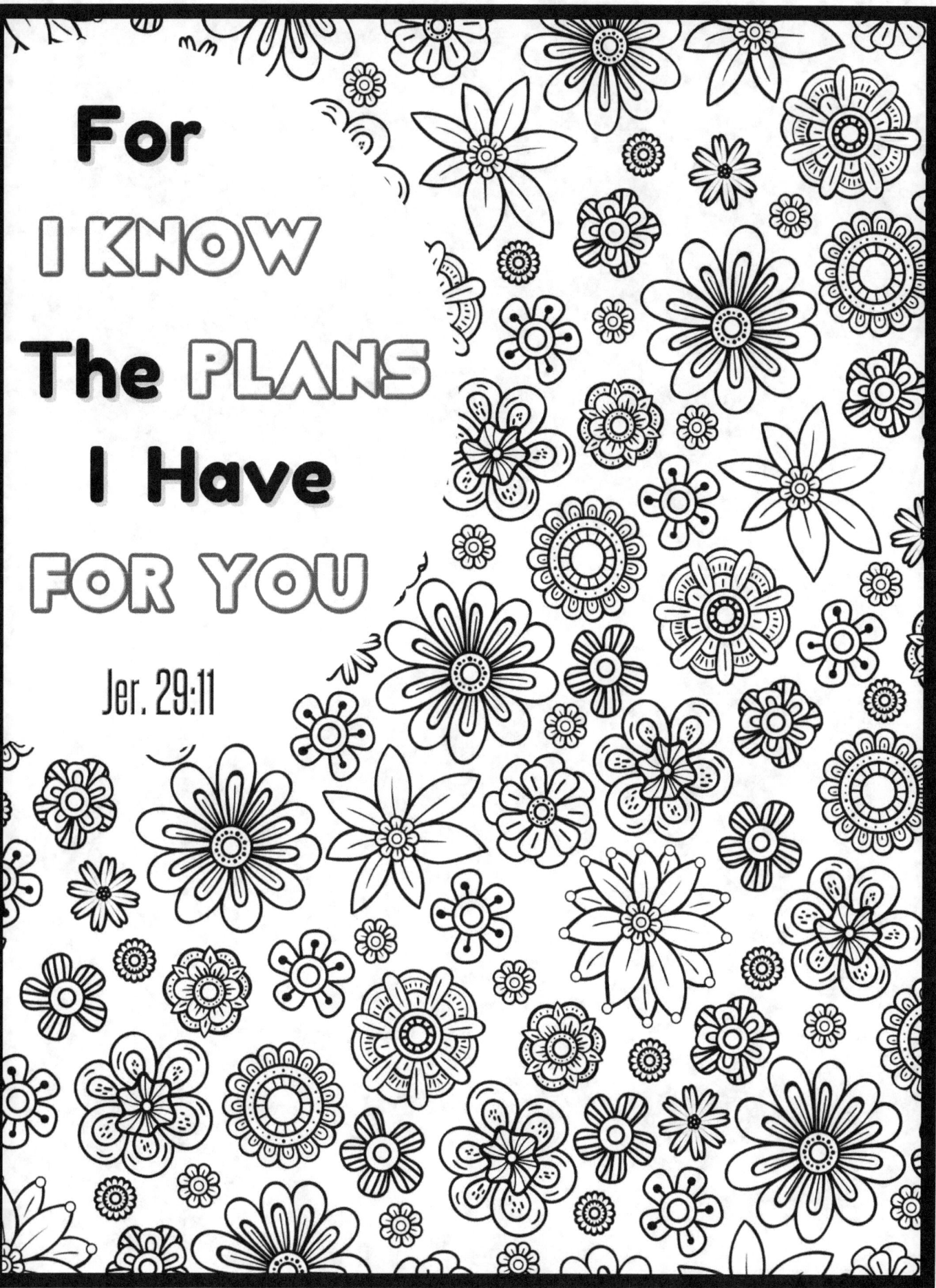

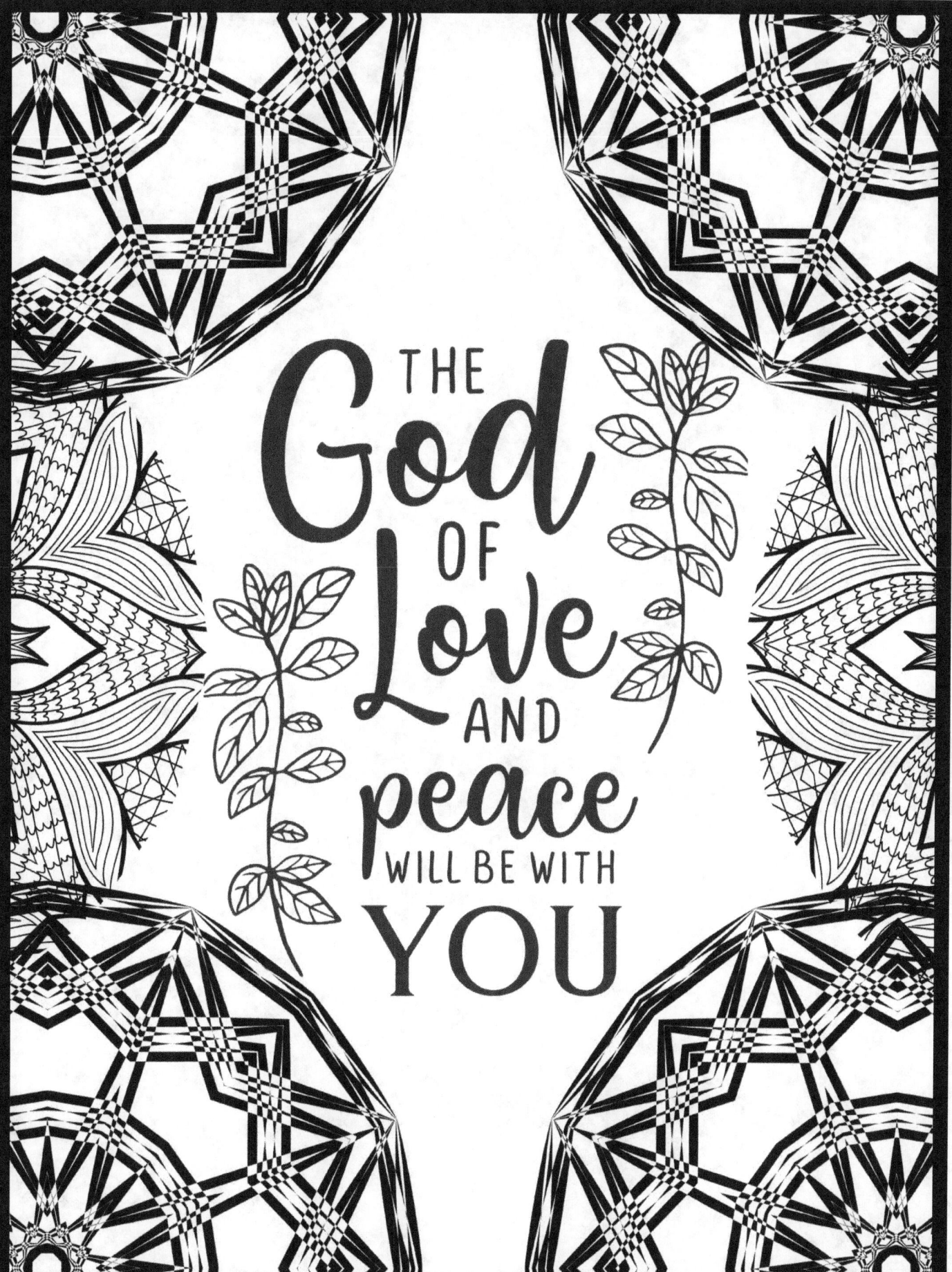

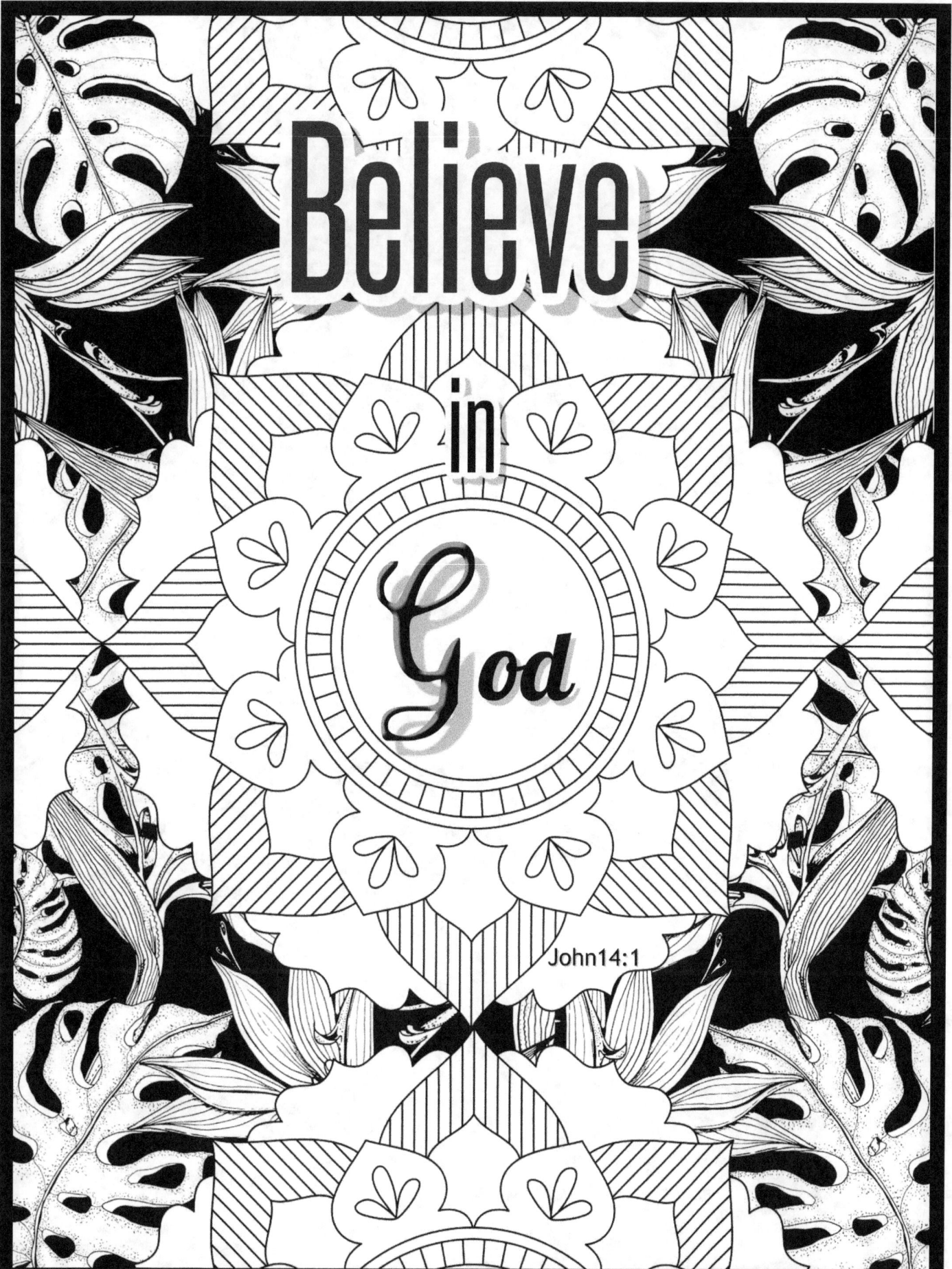

www.ingramcontent.com/pod-product-compliance
Lightning Source LLC
Chambersburg PA
CBHW081659220526
45466CB00009B/2821